Finding Fairies

SECRETS FOR ATTRACTING LITTLE PEOPLE
FROM AROUND THE WORLD

Written by MICHELLE ROEHM McCANN &
MARIANNE MONSON-BURTON

Illustrated by DAVID HOHN

BEYOND
WORDS
Publishing
I N C

DEDICATION

For my sisters, Jamie and Charlotte, who love looking for fairies with me.—Michelle

For those who have tiptoed with me to the "magic casements opening on the foam of perilous seas, in fairy lands forlorn": Becky, Keith, Nathan, and the Monsons.—Marianne

For Moon.—David

We'd like to give a special thanks to all the wonderful people who helped us with research and editing: Meegan Thompson, Erin Doty, Tracy Leithauser, Laura Carlsmith.

Published by
Beyond Words Publishing, Inc.
20827 NW Cornell Road, Suite 500
Hillsboro, Oregon 97124
503-531-8700/1-800-284-9673

ISBN: 1-58270-012-5

Design: Trina Stahl
Proofreader: Susan Beal

Printed in Belgium
Distributed to the book trade by Publishers Group West

Library of Congress Cataloging-in-Publication Data

McCann, Michelle Roehm, 1968-
   Finding fairies : secrets for attracting little people from around the world / by Michelle Roehm McCann and Marianne Monson-Burton ; illustrated by David Hohn.
      p. cm.
   Summary: Describes various types of fairies from around the world and suggests related activities, recipes, and crafts.
    ISBN 1-58270-012-5
    1. Fairies--Juvenile literature. [1. Fairies--Folklore. 2. Folklore. 3. Handicraft.] I. Monson-Burton, Marianne, 1975- II. Hohn, David, 1974- ill. III. Title.

GR549 .M35 2001
398.2--dc21   00-045444

Contents

Introduction

SINCE TIME began, humans have known about the "fairies." In fact, every culture around the world has their own traditions for befriending them. People have discovered favorite fairy treats, songs, games and hiding places. The fairies and the rituals used to attract them are as different and fascinating as the areas they come from—from the tiny winged fairies of South America to the huge and hideous djinn of Arabia.

As fairy lovers ourselves, we have spent years traveling the world collecting stories and activities for this book. In Cairo, we listened to taxi drivers tell of magic lamps and flying carpets. We visited temples in the Yucatan jungle that were built by wise fairy kings. In Africa, we celebrated the friendship of nature sprites in song and dance. We are excited to share the secrets that we discovered with you. Now you can use these traditions to attract fairies from around the world!

So, what exactly *is* a fairy? There are many definitions, but in this book we've focused on magical beings that love and protect nature. Also, we included only those fairies who are friendly to humans—it wouldn't be much fun to attract a nasty fairy, after all.

Although some fairies may come from far away, they have no problem with traveling. So don't worry if you want to attract a fairy from Asia; you're just as likely to find a Chinese house fairy sweeping a floor in Boston as you are in Beijing.

In this book you'll learn to make many different gifts for fairy friends. Leave the presents for them to find, but don't be surprised if the gifts are still around days later. Often fairies take only the "essence" of an object and leave the shell behind (it's simpler to carry that way!).

It was easier for our ancestors to find fairies years ago. Today, as humans take over their wild places, these nature guardians don't trust us like they used to. If you want to find fairies, you must be gentle with the

earth to convince them that you care about their world. You must also be clever. Fairies often appear in disguise. Look carefully—that cat, flower, bird or butterfly could really be a fairy coming to greet you.

However, the greatest fairy-finding secret of all is to believe in them. Because of this, fairies appear most often to children whose imaginations are still open to possibility. Can you imagine what it would be like to float through the air inside a soap bubble, curl up for a nap on the petals of a daffodil, or discover a tiny friend living inside your favorite ring? If you can, the fairies will like you best of all. This book is just for you.

The Mystic Orient— Asia

ASIA IS full of fairies and the stories about them are as ancient as time itself. Some Asian fairies are very powerful and outrageous looking, while others disguise themselves as ordinary humans. Who knows? Maybe someone you know is a fairy!

You would never have to clean your room again if you shared your home with a Chinese house fairy. These industrious creatures love to sweep, scrub, dust, and do all the household chores. At night they tiptoe through neighborhoods and into homes while the humans are sleeping, to choose the families they want to live with. You can entice them to stay at your house by burning incense or leaving an irresistible gift of cinnamon, cherries, peaches, oranges, or white lilies. And be sure that your pots and pans are clean—that's where Chinese house fairies rest for the night.

Chinese fairies are known for their fantastic rewards, which they give to humans who show them kindness. One ancient story tells of a young boy who rescued and cared for a wounded bird. The bird was really a fairy in disguise! When he was well enough to fly again, the grateful bird gave the young hero a pumpkin seed as a reward. The boy thought it was a strange gift, but he planted the seed anyway. When the first pumpkin grew, he cut it open and out poured hundreds of gold coins! So, always be kind to animals . . . they may be fairies in disguise.

Wouldn't you love to have a fairy airport in your house? Chinese house fairies only live in places where they can easily take off and fly at any moment. To entice one of these creatures, your room must be open. If it has lots of sharp corners, posts or beams, a fairy's flight path will be blocked. But you can fix this by putting small mirrors over any trouble spots. Mirrors act as magic doorways for these friendly helpers.

On clear days in the mountains, look for Chinese fairy castles hiding between the tall peaks. And when the moon is full, search the shadows of the lunar landscape for the royal fairy palace called *Kuang-han kung*, the Palace of the Boundless Cold. Its roads are paved with shimmering jade and silver, and the buildings gleam with gold and agate.

IN JAPAN, trees, water, rocks, and even mountains have their own fairy guardians. The Kobito is the easiest Japanese fairy to attract because he adores human food. Look for small holes in the ground near your home— these could be Kobito dwellings. If you put tasty treats near their holes, they may leave you a magic gift in return.

In one Japanese tale, a boy left a sweet dumpling for a Kobito and was given a magic grinder in return. When the grinder's handle

Chinese Cherry Dumplings

THE fairies of China are sure to flock around these delicious cherry dumplings!

WHAT YOU NEED
For cherry mixture:
4 cups pitted red cherries (canned or fresh), ½ cup sugar, 1 Tbs. quick-cooking tapioca

For dumplings:
1 cup flour, ¼ cup sugar, 1 tsp. baking powder, ¼ tsp. salt, ⅓ cup milk, 2 tsp. melted butter

WHAT YOU DO
1. Pour undrained cherries into skillet.
2. Add ½ cup sugar and sprinkle on tapioca.
3. Let stand while preparing dumpling dough.
4. In another bowl sift flour, baking powder, salt, and ¼ cup sugar.
5. Add remaining ingredients and mix lightly to form dough.
6. Bring cherry mixture in the pan to a boil.
7. Drop the dough by tablespoons into the boiling mixture.
8. Cover the skillet and cook for twenty minutes. Serve warm with milk or cream. It will make six dumplings.

was cranked, anything the boy wished for came out! Unfortunately, the boy's wicked brother stole this prize and escaped on a boat. While at sea, he wished for salt to add to his food and white crystals poured out of the magic grinder. Since the brother didn't know how to stop the grinder, his boat filled with salt and sank to the bottom of the sea. There the Kobito grinder sits to this day, churning and churning. That's why the ocean is so salty.

On a crisp winter evening, you might see the Snow Queen walking softly and silently through the moonlit woods. She is the one who brings snow and paints frost on your windows. Her hair and eyes are as black as night and her skin is white like snow.

Another Japanese fairy who lives in untouched woodlands is the Tengu. These tiny nature beings have lovely, iridescent wings and carry sweeping fans. They are guardians of the forest and can disguise themselves as any animal.

Some fairies deserve a bit of caution. While crossing rivers, beware of the Kappa. This dangerous little troll has

Tengu Fairy Fan

WHAT YOU NEED
Construction paper, a tongue depressor, a stapler or glue, and colored pens, glitter, or anything else you want for decorating it

WHAT YOU DO
1. Bend construction paper or posterboard to make a fan shape.
2. Decorate your fan any way you like.
3. Staple or glue it to the end of a tongue depressor.
4. Leave your work of art as a gift for a Tengu on a hot day.

Korean Wrestling Game

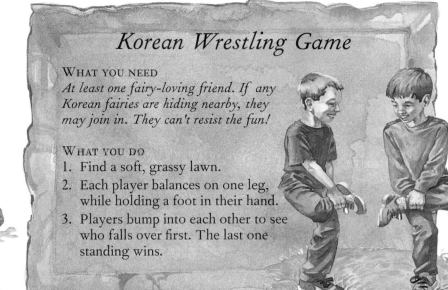

WHAT YOU NEED

At least one fairy-loving friend. If any Korean fairies are hiding nearby, they may join in. They can't resist the fun!

WHAT YOU DO

1. Find a soft, grassy lawn.
2. Each player balances on one leg, while holding a foot in their hand.
3. Players bump into each other to see who falls over first. The last one standing wins.

a head filled with water and tries to drown travelers by bowing down and flooding the river as they cross! But you can trick Kappa if you know his secret. He is extremely polite, so if you bow to him before you cross he will have to bow back. When he does, all the water will pour out of his head and you can get to the other side.

Across the Sea of Japan, the people of Korea know the Tokkaebi. These ugly, mean goblins have just one good quality—they often lose their magic objects. If you happen to find a Tokkaebi club, pound it on the ground and you will receive anything you want. If you find a pointy little Tokkaebi hat, put it on and you will be invisible!

Are you one of those people who hates slugs, snails or anything slimy? It's time to start appreciating these creatures—they may be Korean fairies in disguise. One Korean man found a snail and created a comfy home for it in his water jar. The next day his snail turned into a beautiful fairy-woman who granted his wishes.

The Charming Isles— Great Britain

THESE NORTH Atlantic islands are famous for their fairy legends, which are passed down from generation to generation. In the misty hills, people tell stories of the lovely winged creatures, prankish elves, and industrious gnomes who share their land. You may encounter these flower lovers in groves, forests, and gardens—wherever their favorite blossoms grow.

The forest fairies of England may be glimpsed in the woods, prancing in the moonlight. They often dance in circles, trampling the grass as they go. If you find one of these "fairy rings," especially one encircled with toadstools, you have most certainly found a fairy ballroom. Leave your new friends a gift in the center of the ring. Their favorite delights are milk, jewelry, mirrors, and bread with butter.

If the fairies are very pleased with you, they may invite you to one of their balls. In one British tale, a girl with a beautiful voice wandered through the forest singing. The Fairy Queen was delighted with her melody, so she appeared and took the girl to a magnificent fairy ball.

The girl sang throughout the enchanted evening as the little people danced all around her.

Did you know that May is the official fairy month? On every moonlit May evening, the little people host sumptuous dancing parties attended by fairies dressed in gorgeous gowns. But don't look in the woods for these balls, for they're actually held underwater! To see one of the gala events, look into any pond or lake when the light of the full moon is reflected on its surface. You may glimpse the towers of a fairy kingdom.

On the green moors of Ireland, some fairies live inside hills with cleverly camouflaged doors. These merry creatures love music and if you put your ear to the ground, you may hear fairy melodies drifting up from their castles far below. It is rumored that one famous Irish harpist actually learned his songs while sleeping on a fairy mound. A grassy hill is the perfect place to leave Irish fairy treats like

Marbled Fairy Milk

WHAT YOU NEED
1 cup 2-percent milk, 1 round pie pan, food coloring, liquid dish soap

WHAT YOU DO
1. Pour milk into a pie pan.
2. Add 1-2 drops of different colored food colorings.
3. Drop liquid dish soap into each spot of color and watch the colors chase each other around the pan.
4. Be patient. The longer you watch, the more the colors will move and change.
5. DO NOT DRINK THE MILK! This marbled milk is for fairies only, as the soap will make humans sick. (Keep it away from your pets, too.)

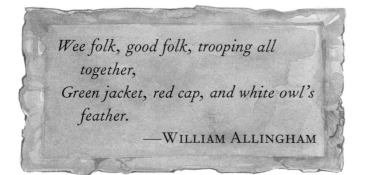

Wee folk, good folk, trooping all together,
Green jacket, red cap, and white owl's feather.

—WILLIAM ALLINGHAM

butter, ribbons, shiny stones, or strawberries and cream.

Don't be surprised if you can't see Irish fairies taking your gift, since they are often invisible. But if you keep your eyes open, you may notice other signs that they are near. If you see flowers bobbing in your garden, they might be bowing graciously to an unseen fairy princess. She could be standing right next to you! And when you feel a sudden gust of wind, it is likely a royal fairy parade passing by. Bow or curtsy to show your respect.

Everyone knows about Leprechauns, but did you know that these Irish elves make all the fairy footwear? The little cobblers work night and day repairing a steady stream of shoes worn out from endless fairy parties.

Because they work so hard, Leprechauns are incredibly rich. Their treasure, however, is not so easy to get. If you discover a Leprechaun's pot of gold, this naughty elf will try to trick you into glancing away just for moment … and then he's gone! But they *can't* disappear as long as you are looking at them, especially if you have a four-leafed clover. If you are clever enough to get the pot of gold, make sure it's the real thing. Leprechauns often give fake gold, which turns to stone overnight.

These little entrepreneurs are not *always* so stingy, however. If a Leprechaun truly likes you, he may formally present you with a leaf or a stone. Don't pass up this simple gift—it could turn into gold overnight.

Irish fairies are famous for their spectacular white horses. The fairies decorate horses with sparkling jewels, silver horseshoes, gold bridles and harps hung in their manes. Then they ride these magnificent animals in a grand fairy procession called the Cavalcade. Can you imagine bejeweled horses the size of kittens parading across your lawn? The few humans who have seen the Cavalcade pass have never forgotten the wondrous sight.

Some people have even gone for ride on fairy horses. Occasionally fairies fall in love with humans and bring them to *Tir-nan-Nog* on the back of a fairy horse. *Tir-nan-Nog* is the Irish fairyland and means "land of the young." The Irish believe it lies to the west, across the sea, and is most easily reached by riding fairy horses over the waves. In this

Lay your ear close to the hill.
Do you not catch the tiny clamour,
busy click of an elfin hammer,
voice of the Leprechaun singing shrill
as he merrily plies his trade?

I caught him at work one day, myself
in the castle ditch where foxglove grows
a wrinkled, wizened, and bearded Elf,
spectacles stuck on his pointed nose,
silver buckles to his hose,
leather apron-shoe in his lap—
rip-rap, tip-tap.

—WILLIAM ALLINGHAM

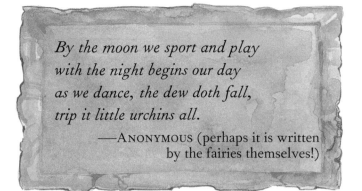

By the moon we sport and play
with the night begins our day
as we dance, the dew doth fall,
trip it little urchins all.

—ANONYMOUS (perhaps it is written
by the fairies themselves!)

If you ever get lost, don't ask a Pixie which way to go. They think it is very funny to point travelers in the wrong direction! Wherever these redheads walk, they leave a trail of glittering gold behind—Pixie dust!

Would you like to host your own Pixie ball? Just sweep your fireplace hearth and decorate it with flowers. This is a favorite Pixie party spot. While you are sleeping, they will be dancing the night away. Be sure to leave a bowl of clean water nearby because fairy moms love to wash their babies while the younger Pixies celebrate.

In the cold Scottish highlands, wee men come out at night to finish human chores. In

blissful land it is forever spring and the fairies dance, sing, and play games all day long. They particularly love a game similar to field hockey, called *hurling,* which is the national sport of Ireland.

"The Londonderry Air"

It is believed that this lovely song was first heard coming from a fairy mound.

Scottish Bannock Cakes

FAIRIES adore these Scottish cakes, especially spread with honey. Once there was a woman who made such wonderful bannocks, the fairies traded gold dust for them!

WHAT YOU NEED
1 cup whole wheat flour, ½ cup white flour, ½ cup oats, 2 Tbs. sugar, 2 tsp. baking powder, ½ tsp. salt, 2 Tbs. melted butter, ⅓ cup raisins or fresh berries, ¾ cup water

WHAT YOU DO
1. Stir together flours, oats, sugar, baking powder, and salt.
2. Add melted butter, raisins, and water.
3. With floured hands, pat dough into a greased pie plate.
4. Bake at 400 degrees for 20-25 minutes until brown.
5. Cut into wedges and spread with butter and honey or dulce de leche.

return for a Brownie's work, leave them a fresh Scottish cake, or *bannock,* spread with honey. They also love cream, so pour a bit over a stone for a delightful treat. Leave your gift near their favorite haunts: castle ruins, streams, groves of trees, lakes, and rocky seashores.

The three-foot-tall Brownies often become particularly attached to one person or family. They especially love little girls with curly golden hair. If a girl has this Brownie-preferred hair, the people of Scotland say it is "the good gift of them that liked her well."

If you listen carefully on a moonlit night, you may hear the faint sounds of bagpipes being played. This is a sure sign that Brownies are close by, for making music is one of their greatest talents. In fact, one famous Scottish piper is said to have learned his instrument from a Brownie when he was a child.

Sand & Sultans— Arabia

JUST BENEATH our world, in the seventh layer of the earth, live the Djinn, which we call genies. A whole chapter in the Koran (the Muslim holy book) is dedicated to the Djinn and tells of their creation from smokeless fire. These Arabian fairies are huge and have horrible, knotted hair and giant teeth, although they sometimes disguise themselves in human form. To discover a Djinn's true identity, ask him, "Are you Ins or are you Djinn?" (*Ins* means human.) If it is a Djinn, don't be afraid—just offer him a piece of gum or a haircut, his favorite gifts, and he will be your ally forever.

Djinn are likely to be found near caves, wells, or cisterns, which are the entrances to their world. One brave Arabian girl climbed down into an empty well and discovered a cavernous marble palace filled with Djinn treasure. She was invited to a legendary Djinn banquet, where guests sat on chairs of gold and were served by dishes that walked around on their own.

Djinn are some of the most powerful fairies in the world. With their magic, they can change themselves into any shape. But lighting a candle will force them to turn back into fairies. They are fond of masquerading as animals, especially black cats and dogs.

Djinn Chewing Gum

WHAT YOU NEED

A handful of whole wheat kernels (you can get these at a health food store), a few drops of corn syrup or a pinch of sugar, peppermint flavoring or ground cloves

WHAT YOU DO

1. Put 10 kernels in your mouth and suck on them until they start to soften. Then chew them. As you chew, they will break apart.
2. Swallow the starch that gets released and keep the solid pieces in your mouth. After you chew for a few minutes, you will have a piece of unflavored gum!
3. Take the gum out of your mouth and roll it in corn syrup or a pinch of sugar for sweetening.
4. Add another small pinch of ground cloves or a drop of peppermint flavoring to make it even tastier. Now you have homemade gum to keep for yourself or give to the Djinn!

Birds are another favorite costume. Who knows? Maybe your pet is a Djinn in disguise! An Egyptian boy once saw someone tormenting a bird with feathers of silver and gold. He rescued the poor creature and discovered it was really a disguised Djinn prince. For his kindness, the boy was rewarded with a magic ring that summoned Djinn to grant his wishes.

Djinn also reward people who are clean, neat and polite. If you manage to impress a Djinn, you will be lucky indeed, for they often grant their human friends all that they desire. Once a poor Arabic girl befriended a Djinn and for the rest of her life, lilies and jasmine fell from her lips whenever she spoke. And every time she took a bath, gold filled the water around her!

Exotic Arabian Perfume

WHAT YOU NEED

Rubbing alcohol, nice-smelling flowers like lavender, rose, mint, jasmine, gardenia, lilac, etc., a small glass bottle with tight-fitting cap or cork (one of your mom's old perfume bottles would work great)

WHAT YOU DO

1. Chop up the flowers and leaves into tiny pieces.
2. Put the flower pieces into your bottle.
3. Add rubbing alcohol until it is almost completely full (but leave room for the cork/cap.)
4. Put on the bottle top and let the perfume sit for two weeks.
5. Strain to remove the flower pieces.
6. If the perfume is not strong enough, let it age one more week. If it still isn't strong enough, add new plant pieces and repeat steps 4-6.
7. Label your perfume bottle and wear your new scent to attract friendly Djinn!

Djinn Treasure Hunt

- Search around your house for a magic carpet. When you stand on it, just say where you want to go and the carpet will take you there!
- Do you have an old lamp in your attic? If it belongs to a Djinn, she will appear when you rub or light the lamp.
- Intricate magic rings are fashioned by the Djinn. They are powerful and lovely. But be careful—whoever wears the ring will become the owner of the Djinn!
- Colored glass perfume bottles may be home to sweet-smelling Djinn. All floral aromas attract these magical creatures.

The Djinn use gold and other precious metals to create exquisite jewelry. These fairies are master craftsmen and no human can copy their intricate, beautiful designs. They also use their magic to create fantastic objects like enchanted wands and trees covered in dancing apples and singing apricots. They can even charm horses so that storms follow in their wake wherever they ride. Although Djinn are powerful, they aren't very smart and often misplace their valuables. If you know what you're looking for, you may find a lost Djinn treasure in your very own house!

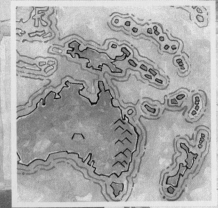

Islands of Fire— Polynesia

SPRINKLED LIKE jewels across vast stretches of the Pacific Ocean, you will find the Polynesian islands. These dots of tropical paradise are actually chains of ancient volcanoes. The local people live in harmony with the aqua blue waves, the swaying lush vegetation, and the sandy beaches that stretch for miles. Because Polynesians live peacefully with the earth, the fairies of these lands are good friends with their human neighbors.

Fairies have lived in Polynesia for thousands of years and every island has its own fairy legend. In the Solomon Islands you may find Bonita Maidens, beautiful water fairies who dress entirely in shells! These kind fairies help local fishermen find their lost hooks. If you see a Bonita Maiden in the ocean, it is a sure sign that you will have a good catch.

The Aboriginal people of Australia believe that fairies control the weather and can predict the future. The European settlers who share this continent brought their own fairies with them from the old world.

The Maori people of New Zealand have learned great secrets from the sea fairies, or Ponaturi. In ancient times the Maoris fished using hooks. Then one dark night a Maori chief hid behind a palm tree to spy on the Ponaturi as they came out from the forest, greeted each other by rubbing noses, and began fishing in the moonlit bay. These fairies fished with something the chief had never seen before.

Through his cunning and wisdom, he was able to capture the strange fairy object, called a kupenga. It was the first fishing net, just like the ones we use today!

Long ago, on the beautiful islands of Hawaii, the playful Menehune fairies lived in peace with humans. But when their enemies, the owls, made war upon them, the Menehune king fled with his followers. They sailed away to the fairy paradise *Pali-Uli*, but a few Menehune didn't want to leave. They stayed behind and lived in the volcanoes, building dazzling palaces out of lava rock. Today you can find these fairies hiding in the mountains, caves, and hollow logs of Hawaii. You will

Menehune Nose-Flute

WHAT YOU NEED
5-7 large leaves, string, scissors

WHAT YOU DO
1. Lay the leaves flat in a small pile. Taro leaves work best, but any large leaves will do.
2. Begin at one end and roll the leaves into a small tube.
3. Tie both ends of the tube with two pieces of string to secure.
4. Cut two small holes in each end of the tube.
5. Your nose-flute is all finished! Don't worry if you can't make beautiful music with your flute . . . the Menehune know exactly how to use these magic instruments. Leave it out for them to find.

recognize them by their earthy red skin and bushy eyebrows. The males have long beards that trail behind them.

These little people definitely know how to have fun. The Menehune celebrate and frolic all night long! If you love to play, these are your kind of fairies! You can find them on moonlit nights dancing to the music of the nose-flute, a magic trumpet made of rolled-up leaves. Menehune also love to wrestle, dive off cliffs, spin tops, fly kites, and race down stony mountains on bamboo sleds. After a night out with these fairies, you are sure to be tired.

Although the Menehune are expert revelers, they are also very hard workers. These little creatures accomplish amazing tasks for people they befriend. Menehune have been known to build huge bridges, dam mighty rivers, and move giant mountains—in a single night!

To thank the Menehune for their favors, humans leave them gifts, usually food. But the Menehune are very picky eaters— their very *favorite* food is shrimp wrapped in taro leaves, but they will also eat gifts of squash, arrowroot, fern frond pudding, angleworms, or fish caught in nets made from morning glory vines. They always eat their food raw because they are afraid of fire.

Luckily for humans who can't find angleworms, the Menehune also adore necklaces. You can create a Menehune necklace by threading shells or flowers on a string. Or use this recipe to make one out of rose petal beads!

Once you have made your gift, wait for a night with a full moon. Leave the necklace outside where moonlight will touch it. Don't be surprised if the beads are still there

Fairy Rose Petal Beads

WHAT YOU NEED

⅔ cup flour, 2 Tbs. salt, ⅓ cup water, 6 cups rose petals, large bowl and spoon, toothpicks, needle and thread.

WHAT YOU DO

1. Mix ⅔ cup flour, salt, and water.

2. Knead until smooth.

3. Tear rose petals into pieces—crumble and crush them.

4. Mix petals into dough, roll dough into beads. Use some extra flour to coat your hands while forming the beads—the dough can get sticky.

5. Push toothpicks through beads to make string holes.

6. Leave toothpicks in and let beads dry for a few hours. Then remove toothpicks and let beads dry for a few days.

7. When completely dry, string beads with thread and needle. Tie ends together to make a beautiful gift for the fairies!

in the morning, because the Menehune collect the shadows of objects. Once a girl left a necklace for the Menehune and hid to see what would happen. They found her gift and held it so that the shadow of the necklace fell upon a leaf. Then they cut out the shadow with a knife, and left the necklace behind!

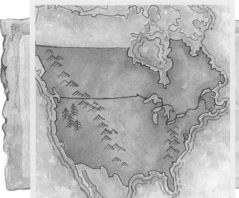

The New World—
North America

*L*ong before white explorers landed on the North American continent, the native people worked and played with nature spirits at their side. American Indian fairies continue to guard and protect the natural world to this day. Although they hide from grown-ups who often mistreat the environment, these fairies love to play with human children.

The mysterious River Elves are bizarre-looking creatures who hide around lakes and rivers in the northeastern areas of the continent. These fairies are hard to miss—their eyes are stacked on top of each other! River Elves make everything out of clay—teepees, balls… even their canoes! You may come across one of their tiny clay creations left at the water's edge.

DO YOU love jumping on leaf piles in the autumn? Next time you do, be careful not to squash a Ja-gen-oh. These tiny Iroquois sprites sleep inside piles of leaves when the weather gets cold. If you scare one out of a nap, it will instantly disguise itself as a dog, butterfly, or blue floating light. If you see one camouflaged as a robin, the Iroquois would say that good news is on the way.

When an Iroquois Indian needs a fairy favor, she will leave a gift for the Ja-gen-oh. The next day, her request will be granted. If you need assistance from the little people, try leaving a Leaf Basket for the friendly Ja-gen-oh.

You may have the secret to becoming invisible right in your own backyard. By rubbing enchanted grass all over their bodies, the Stick Fairies of Idaho make themselves disappear. Perhaps Stick Fairies will leave behind some of this enchanted stuff in your yard. Rub suspicious-looking grass on your arm and see what happens.

The Little People can't become invisible to hide from humans, but they do use an insect disguise to fool us. On late summer evenings, when you hear high-pitched, insect buzzing, you may really be listening to the language of the Little People. These fairies live in lodges that glisten and glow because they're made entirely of insect wings. On stormy nights, they leave their lodges to play pranks on grown-ups! But when they meet human children, they are more likely to start a game of leapfrog.

Another fairy to listen for is the Pah-ho-hoklah. These tiny dwarfs live high in the Cascade Mountains of Oregon, where their bird-like calls echo through the forest. The lovely songs cause the rain to stop, the fog to lift, and the sun to shine!

AMERICAN INDIAN fairies disguise themselves as things many of us would consider

Ja-gen-oh Leaf Basket

WHAT YOU NEED
10 large leaves, a plastic bowl the same size as the basket you want to make, a paintbrush, petroleum jelly, water-based glue (like Elmer's), water

WHAT YOU DO:
1. Turn a plastic bowl upside down—this will be your leaf basket mold.
2. Cover the outside of the bowl with petroleum jelly.
3. Mix 4 parts glue with 1 part water to make a mixture that has the consistency of cream.
4. Stick one layer of leaves onto petroleum jelly, wrapping them around the bowl.
5. Cover leaves with glue mixture using paintbrush (or your fingers) and add another layer of leaves, as if you are doing papier-mâché. The basket should be 2-3 leaves thick.
6. When finished, let the basket dry on the bowl overnight.
7. Carefully remove the basket from the mold.

Fill with fairy presents!

creepy. People who don't know any better see only a harmless spider, but you know it could be an Inktomi fairy in disguise. These little people can turn themselves into eight-legged creatures whenever they want! To get from place to place, Inktomi ride wolves, coyotes and dogs. Does your dog have patches where less hair grows? That could be the spot where an Inktomi sits to ride him.

The Cree Indians of Canada paint beautiful petroglyphs to honor the Mee'megwee'ssio fairies. Along the edges of lakes and rivers you may hear these little

Fairy Rock-Pets

Make a rock-pet and leave it for a friendly Mee'megwee'ssio.

What you need
*a small rock, aluminum foil, ink pens or Fairy Glow Rock Paint (see step 5),
a dab of perfume*

What you do
1. Wrap your rock in tinfoil (or skip to step 4 if you want to use Fairy Glow
   Rock Paint).
2. Decorate your rock any way you want with ink pens—create an animal,
   a ladybug, a flower, or anything you think the fairies will like.
3. Dab your rock-pet with a little perfume.
4. To make Fairy Glow Rock Paint, stir together 2 Tbs. liquid starch, 2 Tbs.
   water, and 1 Tbs. tempura paint in a bowl. Mix in ¼ cup salt and
   paint the mixture on your rock. When the paint dries, your rock
   pet will sparkle like it's covered with fairy dust.

creatures calling to each other. Their voices
sound just like the laughter of human children. They travel the countryside dressed in
gowns made from colored porcupine quills.
Everywhere the Mee'megwee'ssio go, they
carry stones wrapped in silver cloth and
bathed in fine perfumes!

HAVE YOU ever wondered what makes you fall asleep? The Ojibwa Indians believe that the speck-sized Weeng fairies are responsible. These fairies zoom through the air riding on gnats, fireflies, and mosquitoes. They whiz around your room and put you to sleep by whacking you on the head with a tiny club! If you manage to see one before it whacks you into dreamland, the Ojibwa believe that you will have a long, long life.

Another fairy who may share your home is Little Dirt, a friend of Arizona's Hopi Indians. This odd fairy enjoys living in stinky garbage piles! Since he brings good luck to his human hosts, it may be worth leaving a little mess just to have him around. Good luck convincing your parents!

Winter Fairy Feast

WHEN temperatures drop, the fairies and birds that live in cold lands appreciate extra treats! String this Winter Fairy Feast on a tree near your house and let *all* the winged creatures enjoy.

WHAT YOU NEED
a bag of whole cranberries, a bag of peanuts in their shells or popped popcorn, an apple, an orange, a knife, heavy cotton thread, a needle, heavy string or twine

WHAT YOU DO
1. Thread needle with cotton thread (use enough to create a garland the size you like) and tie a knot at the end.
2. Poke needle through the center of your cranberries, peanuts and popcorn, pulling the thread through each, like you're making a necklace.
3. When string is full, you can either tie the ends together to make a circle or leave it as a garland.
4. Slice your apple and orange into ½ inch slices and poke a hole in the middle of each fruit slice.
7. Take as much string or twine as you want and poke it through the holes in each fruit slice. When you've used all your fruit, tie the ends of the twine together, forming a large circle.
8. Hang your garlands and fruit ornaments on a tree outside, just like you're decorating a holiday tree. Let the birds and fairies enjoy!

Ye Olde World— Europe

THE EUROPEAN continent spans the charming castles of Spain, the icy waters of Norway, the sun-drenched islands of Greece, and the snowy steppes of Russia. Its vibrant and varied cultures have countless legends about the magic folk who share their lands.

Down south, Italian fairies called Gianes live in the woods and carry spinning wheels wherever they go. Some people believe they can see the future in those whirring wheels. If you find a piece of cloth spun by the Gianes, it will bring you very good luck.

rising for the night. If you respect nature, you might befriend a Scandinavian Light Elf. These fairies are busy in the springtime, since they make flowers bloom, birds nest, and fruit ripen!

High in the French Alps, fairies who look like small white horses gallop across the icy mountain peaks. They are Lutins, fairies that can change shape whenever they want. They think it is very funny to change into money and watch humans chase after them! Lutins

The fairies of Greece love to play in the boughs of old, knotted olive trees and ride chickens to get from here to there! On the island of Sicily, fairies called Folletti are in charge of changing the weather. They love to whip up windstorms and ride on the howling gales—listen for them laughing gleefully. When they aren't changing the weather, the Folletti ride grasshoppers in a game similar to polo!

From further north in the Netherlands come fairies with bodies so light they are nearly invisible. These creatures travel through the air inside of bubbles! You may also see them dancing in the moonlight on night-blooming flowers.

Off the shores of Scandinavia, magic fairy islands dot the sea. Look out over the ocean as the sun sets and you may see their islands

Pixie Porridge

EUROPEAN fairies love this sweet porridge.

WHAT YOU NEED
1 cup oatmeal, 1 cup boiling water, 1 Tbs. raisins, splash of milk, pat of butter, pinch of sugar, pan

WHAT YOU DO
1. Mix oatmeal, water and raisins in a pan. Bring to a boil over medium heat.
2. Remove from heat and cover for 5 minutes.
3. When oatmeal is hot and ready, add a pat of butter, a splash of milk and a pinch of sugar.

That's just how they love it!

Fairy-Frosted Flowers

FOR fairies who love nature and sweets, this is a perfect treat. DO NOT EAT THEM YOURSELF—most flowers aren't good for humans to eat. Just leave them for the fairies.

WHAT YOU NEED
your favorite flowers, one egg (white only), 1 Tbs. sugar, paintbrush, wax paper

WHAT YOU DO
1. Separate the egg white from the yolk. This is tricky! You may need some help. Throw out the eggshell and yolk.
2. Arrange flowers on wax paper.
3. Dip your paintbrush into the egg white and paint flowers all over.
4. While the flowers are wet and sticky, lightly sprinkle them with sugar.
5. Let flowers dry for 10 minutes. Leave these sparkly treasures anywhere you suspect fairies live.

move from place to place with a little flash of light, like a firefly.

In German-speaking lands, fairies keep fire-breathing dragons as pets. These mysterious fairies live deep in the enchanted Black Forest where trees come alive at night and walk around! German fairies love primroses, which they use as keys to open hidden treasure boxes. Tie several primroses together and touch it to a promising rock. You may discover fairy treasure inside!

When you're in the woods, keep an eye out for Gnomes, which are very common. These small, chubby fairies are kind to humans and help those in need. If you want to attract them, leave gifts of flowers and milk, and keep your cat inside. Cats love to chase Gnomes.

Gnomes and many other European fairies immigrated to the new world with adventurous human explorers. As the great ships crossed the oceans, stowaway fairies hid in human luggage, shoes, and even tucked themselves inside shirt pockets! Duendes, for

Domovoy Soap Carvings

This is a great gift for your bathroom fairies.

WHAT YOU NEED
a bar of soap (any color or kind), a butter knife, a pencil

WHAT YOU DO
1. Use the pencil to draw a design outline onto your bar of soap (a flower or an animal—anything you want).
2. Use the knife to carve around your outline, cutting off the extra soap. Use the knife to carefully shape your animal.
3. Rub water on to smooth out edges and erase your mistakes. Leave next to your tub to share with any Domovoy living nearby.

example, are now common in Latin America, but they originally came from Spain. Even today, Spanish fairies around the world are partial to olives, which grow on twisted old trees in their former homeland.

From Russia comes the Leshy. He is hard to miss with his blue skin, green eyes, and beard. You'll know for sure it's a Leshy if his shoes are on the wrong feet. This clever fellow lives in forests and fields, and can grow or shrink to match the size of plants he's walking through—he can be as small as a blade of grass or as tall as a tree!

The Leshy loves to lead travelers down the wrong path, but he will take you home if you know how to break his spell. Just put your clothes on backwards and your shoes on the wrong feet!

The most common fairies in Russia are the Domovoy. You may not realize one lives near you because they disguise themselves as big, messy cats or even piles of hay, but you'll know they're around if you hear their whispers. You can lure one into your house by leaving a treat for them under your stove—they love bread and milk.

Domovoy are useful to have around because they help with chores and make noise if danger is approaching. If one decides to live with you, make sure to leave a bit of water and soap in the tub occasionally, so it can bathe. Otherwise it will soon stink up your house!

Be careful with Domovoy in March. This is when they shed their winter skin (like a snake!) and grow new, lighter ones for the summer—it makes them very grumpy! Let your friend sulk in peace during this time.

Russian Lullaby

WHEN a Domovoy lives in your house he may help you fall asleep. He places his hands over your sleepy eyes and sings:

Sleep, my baby, sleep now and rest,
Safe as a fledgling in its wee nest.
Sleep now and rest, safe in your nest.
Sleep, my baby, sleep.

Land of Spices—India

THE PEOPLE of India have believed in fairies for thousands of years. On Hindu holy days like *Diwali* and *Holi,* these tiny, playful fairies come out and celebrate with humans, bringing them happiness and good luck. Indian children often search around the trunks of pine trees for the greenish-blue sprites who live there. On hot summer nights, the fairies can be found dancing on moonlit flowers and vines.

Sticky sweet, sugary foods are the favorite delight of Indian fairies. At parties they eat more dessert and candy than you can possibly imagine. The hungriest fairies of all are called Mazikeen. Since they don't need to sleep, work, or go to school, these little people throw parties and play all day long! If you receive an invitation to one of their parties, be sure to bring lots of candy and don't expect to get home early.

While the Mazikeen party the night away, the Lesidhe fairies prefer a more tranquil lifestyle. They are the ancient guardians of the forest, so you must be kind to nature if you want these wilderness protectors for friends. Lesidhe are difficult to find because they live alone in the deepest parts of the woods, and can disguise themselves as plants, leaves, and animals. On quiet mornings and evenings, listen for the call of a mockingbird. It could be a Lesidhe trying to throw you off its track.

ONCE A poor Indian man fell asleep under a banyan tree with his last bowl of cold rice. The tree was home to some very hungry Vanadevatai fairies who ate all the rice while he slept. They loved the bland meal because it was

Mazikeen Rock Candy

WHAT YOU NEED
4 cups sugar, 1 cup water, string, pencil, glass jar, saucepan, spoon, food coloring (optional)

WHAT YOU DO
1. Pour 1 cup water and 2 cups sugar into pan.
2. Heat on medium (do not boil), stirring constantly until sugar dissolves. Gradually add 2 more cups sugar and stir until it dissolves.
3. Remove from heat and pour into a glass jar.
4. Stir in a few drops of food coloring.
5. Tie string to pencil, place pencil over mouth of jar so string hangs down into liquid. Sugar crystals will begin forming on string in a few hours.
6. The next day, pull string out of jar to check out your crystals. To make your crystals bigger, reheat leftover liquid and repeat steps 3, 5 and 6. Repeat until your rock candy has grown as big as you want it. Eat it or share it with the sweet-toothed Mazikeen fairires.

so different from the fancy food they usually ate.

To repay him for the special treat, they left him two empty bowls. When he awoke and discovered his rice was gone, the man angrily pounded the empty bowls on the ground. Suddenly, servants appeared carrying steaming bowls of scrumptious food! To celebrate, the kind man held a feast and invited everyone in his village, rich and poor.

His greedy neighbor was jealous, so he also left food for the Vanadevatai at their banyan tree. He also received two bowls and planned a huge party; but *his* party was only for the rich and important people of the village. At the feast, he banged his magic bowls on the ground and dozens of huge men appeared. Instead of dishing out delicious food, they grabbed all the guests and shaved their heads bald!

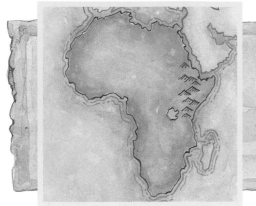

Africa—The Vast Continent

AFRICA IS the second biggest continent on Earth—it's three times as big as the United States! There are modern cities, vast deserts, thundering waterfalls, thriving villages, and broad savannas where lions, giraffes, and elephants roam. Africa includes dozens of different countries and even more cultures, each with their own unique beliefs, traditions, and stories about fairies.

In many African stories the fairies masquerade as animals that can talk. The Fan people of West Africa, for instance, share their rivers with crocodiles and believe these reptiles are actually magic beings in disguise. To show their respect and to keep the crocodile fairies happy, the Fan people leave gifts along the riverbanks.

In the country of Swaziland, they tell the story of a beautiful princess named Kitila. When her father died, Kitila's uncle became the new king. He was jealous of his niece, so he put a spell on her turning her into a horrible monster! All the villagers were terrified—they ran away from Kitila and refused to give her food. As the monster-princess sat crying beside a lake, a sympathetic fairy gave her a carved stick. Carrying the magic staff, she walked into the water and the curse fell away. Hundreds of little fairies flocked around her, bringing her delicious foods to feast on!

A noble prince caught sight of Kitila feasting with the fairies. It was love at first sight. When she stepped out of the water, she turned back into a monster. But the prince still wanted to marry her because he had seen the kindness in her heart. Kitila agreed to be his bride and on the morning of her wedding day she went to bathe with the fairies. As she entered the lake, the awful spell slipped into

Fairy Rattle

WHAT YOU NEED
20 halved walnut shells (available at craft stores), nail, wire, ink pens (optional)

WHAT YOU DO
1. You can decorate your walnut shells with ink pen first, if you want. Traditional African colors are black, red, green, and yellow.
2. Make a small hole in each walnut shell with the tip of a nail.
3. String the walnut shells onto a length of wire.
4. Loop the wire into a small circle large enough to fit your hand through. Twist the ends together to close the circle (be careful of the sharp ends).

Now you have your own African fairy instrument! Shake to make beautiful noise.

the water. The fairies grabbed the spell and flew it far, far away. Kitila looked like a human princess once more. She married the prince and . . . well, you know the rest!

Wherever you hear African stories like this one being told, you'll probably hear drumming as well. The drum is the world's oldest instrument and many Africans believe it has special power to attract fairies. Little sprites love listening to the thump and rattle of noise-makers—talking drums, medicine drums, hand drums, baskets of dried corn, bells, rattles and even sticks. In the forests and on the savannas, they can be found dancing to the irresistible rhythms.

Masks also attract African fairies and are used during celebrations. The masks are carved into animal shapes—gazelles, monkeys, lions, hyenas, and birds—and give protection to whoever wears them! Long ago in Mali, a half-human and half-antelope fairy

African Masks

FOR a real African fairy celebration, wear this mask while you dance and shake your fairy rattle!

WHAT YOU NEED
Cardboard or poster board, scissors, tongue depressor, stapler or string and ink pens, glue, glitter, paint, beads, string, macaroni, or any other things for decoration.

WHAT YOU DO

1. Choose a mask shape on this page. These masks are from Congo, Uganda, and Tanzania.

2. Fold a piece of scratch paper in half lengthwise and draw the outline of half of your mask shape. Cut along the line. When you unfold the cut paper, you'll have a symmetrical mask pattern.

3. If you do not want to wear your finished mask, skip to step 4. If you do want to wear it, hold the pattern up to your face and mark where the eyes and mouth should go (have someone else help you with this so you don't poke yourself in the eye). Cut out eye and mouth holes.

4. Put your paper pattern on your cardboard and trace around outside edges and the eye and mouth holes.

5. Cut your finished mask out of the cardboard.

6. Decorate your mask with the materials you have chosen.

7. To wear your mask you can staple string to both sides of the mask (just above your ears) and tie behind your head. To hold your mask in front of your face, glue or staple a tongue depressor to the bottom of the mask as a handle.

8. To hang your mask, poke a hole in the top of it, put string through the hole and tie the ends together creating a loop. Voilà—it's ready for the wall.

taught the Bamana people how to till the fields and plant the crops. To this day, the people of Mali thank their fairy friend by wearing antelope masks during their harvest celebrations.

In Ghana, monkey-sized sprites called Asamanukpai dance on outcroppings of quartz stone. As the playful creatures prance about, their feet polish the stone to a brilliant shine. Even now, Ghana is filled with mysterious stones that have holes worn right through the middle. Many people wonder how the holes got there, but you know it's from endless fairy dancing.

If you find one of their dancing stones, it is the perfect place to leave a fairy gift such as sweet fruit, yams, dolls, or clean water. In one story from Ghana, a spider needed a fairy favor. To catch an Asamanukpai, he put a bowl of yams and a doll beneath an Odum tree. The fairies were so delighted with his gifts that they flocked all around him and granted his wish. If the Asamanukpai like your gift and befriend you, they may squeeze fairy juice into your eyes, ears, and mouth. The magic liquid will give you the power to read people's minds, see the future, and sing with the fairies.

Tanzanian Baked Bananas

THESE bananas are a favorite fairy treat from Tanzania.

WHAT YOU NEED
2 large unpeeled bananas
2 Tbs. butter
½ cup brown sugar
1 tsp. cinnamon
1 tsp. lemon juice
shallow baking dish

WHAT YOU DO
1. Wash the bananas and cut ends off. DO NOT PEEL.
2. Put the bananas in a baking dish.
3. Bake at 350 degrees for 10 minutes.
4. Turn the bananas over and cook 10 more minutes.
5. In a small pan, mix the other ingredients and cook over medium heat until it starts to bubble.
6. Remove bananas from oven, peel (Careful! They're hot), and pour sauce on top. Mmm . . . delicious!

Latin Fiesta—Central & South America

Ancient ruins, steamy jungles, tropical islands, and towering mountains—all are found in the Latin world. And the fairies of these regions are as exotic as the plants and animals that fill the famous rainforests!

The next time a rainstorm ruins your plans, why not search for Mexican Aires? These incredible fairies are made entirely of gleaming, glistening water! Most of the time they live quietly at the bottom of rivers, pools, and waterfalls, where they blend perfectly with their surroundings. They collect barrels of clouds, rain, snow, hail, lightning, and thunder, and are anything but quiet when they dump their collection on unsuspecting humans! Severe storms are actually fierce Aires battles. On non-rainy evenings when these fairies are at home, watch as the sun sets over water. If you see thousands of tiny lights sparkling in the ripples, that's an Aires village!

One Mayan legend tells of an old woman who lived in the jungle. One day a snake brought her a strange spotted egg, which she

Mexican Fairy Flowers

LEAVE this colorful bouquet for Mexican fairies, or use it to brighten up your own table.

WHAT YOU NEED
Flower-colored tissue paper in 12 inch x 12 inch squares, green pipe cleaners, scissors

WHAT YOU DO
1. Cut tissue paper into circles with wavy edges. Make the circles different sizes.
2. Layer the pieces of tissue paper together, putting the largest on the bottom and the smallest on the top of the pile.
3. Poke two holes about 1 inch apart, in the center of the pile.
4. Put pipe cleaner through one hole, bend in the middle, and thread through the other hole (like a button).
5. Twist the two ends of the pipe cleaner together to make a stem. The tissue will crinkle into a flower shape!

took care of for months. Finally, the egg hatched and a tiny boy climbed out! The elf child was no bigger than a tree frog, but the woman loved him and taught him the ways of the forest. He didn't grow much bigger, but he became very wise.

Soon villagers were traveling to the jungle to ask the "Dwarf Wizard" for advice. He became so famous that the village king grew jealous and commanded him to build a stone temple as big as his royal palace . . . in just one night! If the boy could do it, he could be king; if not, he would die.

It was an impossible task, but the Dwarf Wizard asked his animal friends for help. Hundreds of jaguars, monkeys, toucans, sloths, and insects came to his rescue. With their help (and a little bit of fairy magic), the giant pyramid was built by sunrise. It was even taller and more magnificent than the king's temple!

The Dwarf Wizard became the new ruler and was wise and kind to the villagers. To teach the mean-hearted king a lesson, the Dwarf Wizard assigned him to care for the children of the village. He knew they would teach the grumpy king how to love again. Even today you can see the "Dwarf's House" towering above the steamy Yucatan jungle, reminding visitors of the power of kindnes— and the magic of fairies!

From the tropical island of Bermuda come shy dwarves who look like tiny red-haired apes! To find them, look for their bizarre footprints. Their feet point backwards and their big toe sticks out to the side. These forest dwellers adore exotic fruits and nuts.

Cool Caribbean Crush

FAIRIES of the Caribbean will appreciate this cool drink made from their favorite fruits.

WHAT YOU NEED
1 peeled banana, ½ cup orange juice, ¼ cup pineapple chunks or rings, 5 ice cubes, blender

WHAT YOU DO
1. Combine ingredients in blender.
2. Blend on high for a minute until smooth.

Ekkekko is such a popular dwarf that almost every family in Bolivia has a statue of him. Like Santa Claus in Europe and North America, Ekkekko adores bringing presents to humans and even has his own holiday. Each year, people decorate statues of Ekkekko with miniatures of objects they would like to receive: shoes, money, food, and even tiny houses and cars!

You may think Ekkekko looks pretty funny covered in all that junk, but even stranger looking is Anchanchu. This big-bellied Bolivian dwarf has a tail and pointy goat feet. He dresses like a Spanish soldier in a wide-brimmed silver hat, and rides around on a pig! You'll know Anchanchu's coming because he creates whirlwinds, sleet, and hail wherever he goes. He has hoards of gold and silver, which he may share with you if you don't laugh at his ridiculous appearance.

If you want to lure a Brazilian fairy, you should learn to play the flute. The Jakui adores this instrument so much that he will make his home inside your flute and help you create enchanting music!

The most common fairy in all of Central and South America is the Duende. These dwarfs are originally from Spain, but hundreds of years ago they sailed across the Atlantic with Spanish conquistadors. Duendes in each Latin American country are unique—in Argentina they are covered in polka dots, in Costa Rica they have pointy ears and wear berets, and in other areas they smell like chicken droppings!

Anchanchu Lure

ALL across Bolivia the landscape is littered with *anchanchus*, small piles of rocks built by humans to attract this wealthy fairy. Anchanchu lures will be most effective if you top them with his favorite treat. Any kind of corn will do: corn on the cob, corn tortillas, corn chips, etc.

WHAT YOU NEED
smooth rocks, corn products of any kind

WHAT YOU DO
1. Make a round pile of smooth stones.
2. Put the tasty corn snack on top.
3. Sit back and wait for Anchanchu's arrival.

Duende Dulce de Leche

IN Argentina this butterscotch-type sauce is served on bread, ice cream, and cookies.

WHAT YOU NEED
1 can sweetened condensed milk, saucepan, and water

WHAT YOU DO
1. Shake up a can of condensed milk very well.
2. Place unopened can in saucepan and cover completely with water.
3. Boil for 1½ hours, replacing water if you need to.
4. Dump water and can out into sink (be careful, it is very hot!)
5. Let can sit for an hour or put it in the refrigerator until it is completely cool.
6. Open with can opener and spoon onto your favorite treat.

The original nature lovers, Duendes live in isolated, pristine areas. You may find one guarding the forest, jungle, or even a single tree. The best time to see these fairies is at night, but they also come out during the heat of the day when humans take their "siestas." The Duendes of Argentina will only visit your house if it's clean, but in other countries they will only come if it's messy! Either way, you can always tempt Duendes with food. In Peru they sip molasses, in Panama they are fish-lovers, and in Argentina they love the sweet treat Dulce de Leche.

These dwarfs are usually invisible to adults, but children can see them clearly. They can even make *you* invisible if they touch you! Duendes disguise themselves as just about anything. A whirlwind, shadow, coconut, spider, stick, bird, or dog might be a Latin fairy in disguise. Sometimes they change into cats so it's easy to sneak into your house and sleep by a warm fire. Hmm, maybe that stray cat slinking around is really a Duende!

Throw a Fantastic Fairy Party

FAIRIES LOVE to have a good time, especially with children like you. You can celebrate almost any occasion by throwing your own fairy party. If you fill your party with fairy attractions, you and your friends will have a great time, and you never who else may show up to surprise you!

Fairy Invitations: The invitations should have your favorite fairies on them, of course! You can make the invitations yourself with colored paper, markers, and glitter. Write on each card that the party will be "in honor of the fairies." You might also include a fairy poem from this book on the invitation.

Fairy Decorations: Be creative and decorate your house like a fairy palace. Be sure to use decorations that fairies adore such as flowers, streamers, balloons, confetti, and your own fairy artwork. Sprinkle the table with Sugar-Frosted Flowers. Make Mexican Fairy Flowers for your guests and set them at each table setting with their name attached. When your guests arrive, they can twist the flower stems to make bracelets or to weave into their hair.

Fairy Costumes: You may want to ask your friends to come dressed as fairies. Be creative! Put flowers in your hair, decorate your eyes with body glitter, and wrap a stick in tinfoil to make a magic wand. Now that you know so many fairies from around the world, you should be able to create a unique fairy costume for yourself. Clothes made from shiny, silky fabric can easily be turned into fairy outfits just by adding wings.

A Party

In Honor of the Fairies

Fairy Foods: Serving fairy food is a sure way to attract the little people to your party. You and your friends could make Duende Dulce de Leche and put it on ice cream or cookies, Tanzanian Baked Bananas, Chinese Cherry Dumplings, Arctic Snow Cones, and Cool Caribbean Crush for drinks. All of these sweet treats taste great with party foods such as pizza, burgers, and hot dogs.

Fairy Activities: If it's a nice day, try some exciting fairy activities outside. The Korean Wrestling Game is lots of fun for a big group. Or why not build a majestic fairy palace for your little friends? You and your guests can use sticks and rocks for the walls and floor, large leaves for the roof, and moss for the carpet. Fill your house with fairy gifts from this book and see who comes to visit.

If the rain keeps you indoors, you and your friends can still have a magical time. Use face paint to draw your guests' favorite fairies on their faces. And you can still create a fairy palace—just build one out of a cardboard box. Use old fabric for the roof, a colorful scarf for a rug, and jewelry boxes for comfy beds. Just think how happy your house fairies will be!

Fairy Wings

GET an adult to help you make your fairy wings.

WHAT YOU NEED
2 metal hangers, 1 pair old nylons (white or colored nylons look best), 2 safety pins, and 2 strips of cloth (1 inch wide by 2 feet long). Glue, glitter, ink pens, and sequins (optional).

WHAT YOU DO
1. Hold both hangers so the hooks cross each other. Twist the hooks around each other so that the hangers stick together. Bend the ends of the hooks so that nothing pokes out. The hangers should now look like the outline of two fairy wings.
2. Pull each nylon leg over a hanger and wrap remaining nylon around hanger hooks and pin with safety pins.
4. Decorate the wings with pens, glue and glitter.
5. Make two loops out of the cloth strips and tie them to the middle of your wings. The loops should be big enough to fit your arms through. Voilà—you're a fairy!

Pixie Dust

BUY small jars of gold glitter at a craft store. On plain paper write "PIXIE DUST" in swirling, magical letters. Glue your finished labels to the jars for a magical present. Tell your guests to leave their jar out on a moonlit night for fairies to charm.

Fairy Party Favors: Your guests will enjoy treats they can take home after your party. The Tengu Fairy Fan, Fairy Rock-Pet, Crystal Rock Candy, and Pixie Dust make great party favors.

Grow a Gorgeous Fairy Garden

*F*AIRIES LOVE nature in general, but they are particularly drawn to flowers. Sometimes these flowers are useful to the fairies, or sometimes they just enjoy curling up inside a blossom to sleep the day away. Whether it's in your backyard or in a windowbox garden, here are some ideas to help you make your own fairy-friendly space.

Bluebells: British legend says that fairies are summoned to their midnight dances by the ringing of the bluebells.

Daisies: Wearing a daisy chain will protect you from fairy pranks.

Foxglove: Fairy hats and gloves are made from foxglove. Look closely and you will see tiny spots on the blossoms—these are fairy fingerprints!

Jasmine: The scent of this flower attracts fairies from China, India, and Arabia.

Marigolds: To see invisible fairies, pick a marigold, mix it with water, and dab a few drops on your eyelids.

Pansy: Fairies use this blossom to make powerful love potions.

Primroses: If you put primroses on your doorstep, fairies will be able to enter your house and bless you while you sleep.

Pussywillows: The soft silky pods are used as pillows by all kinds of little sprites.

Rocks: Shiny stones like marble and agate attract fairies, so use them for borders or paths in your fairy garden.

Mirrors: Fairies love looking at their own reflections. Put a mirror in a special spot in your garden.